When Jesus' Friends Betrayed Him

Words by Norman C. Habel
Pictures by Jim Roberts

A PURPLE PUZZLE TREE BOOK

COPYRIGHT © 1973 CONCORDIA PUBLISHING HOUSE, ST. LOUIS, MISSOURI
CONCORDIA PUBLISHING HOUSE LTD., LONDON, E. C. 1
MANUFACTURED IN THE UNITED STATES OF AMERICA
ISBN 0-570-06547-X

Concordia Publishing House

What would you do if you knew
you only had three days to live?
Where would you go?
Whom would you see?
And what would your last wish be?

When Jesus' death was very near,
He didn't run away.

First He visited the house
of a man called Simon the leper.
He ate a meal with him
to show His love for lonely men
that other people would not touch.

A lonely lady sat on the floor
and listened to Jesus that day.
Deep down in her heart she sang
the song that lonely people pray:

    Why am I lonely and why do I weep
    for someone who won't run away?
    Where are the friends who enjoyed
    my love?
    Oh, why is the morning so gray?

    Friends who betray me are everywhere,
    like seaweed thrown up on the shore.
    Will this Man forgive me and love
    me as me?
    In this life I ask nothing more.

Then slowly the lonely lady rose
and walked up close to Jesus,
as people gasped and stared.
She took a jar of precious ointment.
She gently broke the little jar
and poured the oil on Jesus' head
as perfume filled the air.

"What a terrible waste of money,"
the jealous disciples whispered.
"We might have sold this jar of oil
and given a gift to the poor."

"Leave the girl alone," said Jesus.
"She did a beautiful thing.
She gave Me all the love she had
and anointed My body for burying.
She will always be My friend."

Now Judas was the joker
among all of Jesus' friends.
For Judas' heart was full of greed,
and he wanted more than Jesus' love.

So Judas went to see the priests
who wanted Jesus dead.
"What will you give for Jesus?"
Judas the joker asked.
"Thirty pieces of silver," they said.
"That's the price for a slave!"

A little while later
Jesus and all His disciples
sat down to eat the Passover meal.
And during that meal they remembered
how God delivered His people from Egypt
and saved them all from death.

Then Jesus said, "My friends!
Will you really be My friends?"

Then Jesus started singing softly:
    Friends who are true are as hard to find
    as diamonds and pearls in the sea.
    I know in My heart as I eat with you all
    that someone will soon betray Me.

"Is it I? Is it I?
Will I betray you?"
said each of the sad disciples.
Well, Judas was the joker,
and soon he left the room
to betray his own best Friend.

Then Jesus broke a loaf of bread
and sang a song of thanks like this
for all of us to hear:
    This is My body I'm breaking for you
    like grains of wheat in the sun.
    Eat it and find here the Love of God
    that heals you and makes you all one.

Then Jesus took a cup of wine
and sang a song of thanks like this
for all of us to hear:
    This is My blood I am shedding for you
    to bring you forgiveness of sin.
    Drink it and find here the love of God
    that gives you a new life within.

And that's the meal God's people enjoy
when they come to His table in church,
where Christ Himself is present
to give us all His life and love.

After that very special meal
Jesus went to the Mount of Olives,
and on the way said, "Friends!
Before this night is over
you'll all desert Me too."

"Never! Never! Never!"
said Old Rock the fisherman,
"I'll never let You down."

"Oh, yes, you will," said Jesus.
"Before the cock crows twice
you will deny Me thrice."

They rested in a garden
until Judas the joker appeared.
He brought a bunch of tough guys
with swords and clubs and spears.

Slowly Judas came to Jesus
and kissed Him on the cheek,
as any friend might do.
For that kiss was the sign
for the tough-looking guys
to drag Jesus off to the priests.

Then Old Rock the fisherman
swung his sword around
like a flying fishing net.
He sliced the ear off one tough guy
and swung his sword again.

But Jesus stopped his swinging
and healed the tough guy's ear.
"It has to be this way," said Jesus.
"I go to My death from here."

When they dragged Jesus away,
none of His friends went with Him.
Jesus went all alone!

Then Jesus was taken to Caiaphas,
the proud and pompous old high priest,
who asked a hundred questions:
"Are You the Son of God?" he said.
"You said it!" Jesus replied.
"But one day you will see Me again
  riding the clouds of the sky."

"For that," the high priest shouted,
"You must be put to death.
  You claim to be God Himself."

While they asked these questions of Jesus,
Old Rock crept into the courtyard
and warmed himself by the fire.

Then one of the maids in the courtyard
said, "You are a friend of Jesus,
that clown from Galilee."

"Never! No! Never!" said Rock,
"I don't even know the man."

The maid then spoke to people nearby,
"I'm sure this big fisherman
followed that Jesus around."

"Never! No! Never!" said Rock,
"I don't even know the man."

Then one of the others nearby
said, "You! You must be His friend.
You even talk like that clown."

"Never! No! Never!" said Rock,
"I don't know the man at all!"

Just then a rooster crowed twice,
and Rock remembered the words of
his Lord,
"Before the cock crows twice,
you will deny Me thrice."

Old Rock went out and wept aloud.
He too had betrayed his Friend,
the best Friend a man could have.
And now that Friend was about to die,
and Rock didn't understand
that Jesus would die for you and for me
according to God's puzzle plan.

As Rock went off into the night
this song must have rung in his ears:

Friends who betray me are everywhere
like seaweed thrown up on the shore.
Will this Man forgive me and love me
as me?
In this life I ask nothing more.

OTHER TITLES

SET I
WHEN GOD WAS ALL ALONE 56-1200
WHEN THE FIRST MAN CAME 56-1201
IN THE ENCHANTED GARDEN 56-1202
WHEN THE PURPLE WATERS CAME AGAIN 56-1203
IN THE LAND OF THE GREAT WHITE CASTLE 56-1204
WHEN LAUGHING BOY WAS BORN 56-1205
SET I LP RECORD 79-2200
SET I GIFT BOX (6 BOOKS, 1 RECORD) 56-1206

SET II
HOW TRICKY JACOB WAS TRICKED 56-1207
WHEN JACOB BURIED HIS TREASURE 56-1208
WHEN GOD TOLD US HIS NAME 56-1209
IS THAT GOD AT THE DOOR? 56-1210
IN THE MIDDLE OF A WILD CHASE 56-1211
THIS OLD MAN CALLED MOSES 56-1212
SET II LP RECORD 79-2201
SET II GIFT BOX (6 BOOKS, 1 RECORD) 56-1213

SET III
THE TROUBLE WITH TICKLE THE TIGER 56-1218
AT THE BATTLE OF JERICHO! HO! HO! 56-1219
GOD IS NOT A JACK-IN-A-BOX 56-1220
A LITTLE BOY WHO HAD A LITTLE FLING 56-1221
THE KING WHO WAS A CLOWN 56-1222
SING A SONG OF SOLOMON 56-1223
SET III LP RECORD 79-2202
SET III GIFT BOX (6 BOOKS, 1 RECORD) 56-1224

SET IV
ELIJAH AND THE BULL-GOD BAAL 56-1225
LONELY ELIJAH AND THE LITTLE PEOPLE 56-1226
WHEN ISAIAH SAW THE SIZZLING SERAPHIM 56-1227
A VOYAGE TO THE BOTTOM OF THE SEA 56-1228
WHEN JEREMIAH LEARNED A SECRET 56-1229
THE CLUMSY ANGEL AND THE NEW KING 56-1230
SET IV LP RECORD 79-2203
SET IV GIFT BOX (6 BOOKS, 1 RECORD) 56-1231

SET V
THE FIRST TRUE SUPER STAR 56-1242
A WILD YOUNG MAN CALLED JOHN 56-1243
THE DIRTY DEVIL AND THE CARPENTERS BOY 56-1244
WHEN JESUS DID HIS MIRACLES OF LOVE 56-1245
WHEN JESUS TOLD HIS PARABLES 56-1246
OLD ROCK THE FISHERMAN 56-1247
SET V LP RECORD 79-2204
SET V GIFT BOX 56-1248

SET VI
WONDER BREAD FROM A BOY'S LUNCH 56-1249
WHEN JESUS RODE IN THE PURPLE PUZZLE
   PARADE 56-1250
   WHEN JESUS' FRIENDS BETRAYED HIM 56-1251
   THE DEEP DARK DAY WHEN JESUS DIED 56-1252
   DANCE, LITTLE ALLELU, WITH ME 56-1253
   THE KEY TO THE PURPLE PUZZLE TREE 56-1254
   SET VI LP RECORD 79-2205
   SET VI GIFT BOX 56-1255

the PURPLE PUZZLE TREE